The Successful Truck Own

2018 EDITION

A Business Guide
For The Start-Up
Independent Owner Operator

The Successful Truck Owner Operator

A BUSINESS MANUAL FOR

THE INDEPENDENT

Start-UP

OWNER OPERATOR

BY   J.W. LESSING

Table of Contents

Introduction

Dear Trucking Partner:

Congratulations on your decision to start your own business in the trucking industry. The success of the American economy depends on enterprising men and women like you who make their living in this field.

The independent truck owner-operator faces a unique and challenging business environment as (s)he conducts business on the open road from a truck that not only serves as an office, but also as a second home.

Motivation and hard work alone will not guarantee success. You have to possess business skills, technical knowledge and industry experience to succeed as an owner-operator.

Our business manual will guide you through the process of get- ting started in trucking. Then it will show you how to develop a business plan and how to successfully manage your day-to-day operations. Finally, it will explain why and how you can obtain your own operating authority.

Thank you for choosing our publication "The Successful Truck Owner Operator."

Best wishes for a successful future,

J.W. Lessing

Getting Started

Trucks transport 94 percent of all consumer, 77 percent of all industrial, and 68 percent of all farm goods in the United States, according to the U.S. Department of Transportation. Annually, the value of all goods shipped exceeds $6 trillion.

You are excited about your career decision, but please proceed with caution and prudence. Owning and operating an 18-wheeler requires research and planning.

As an owner-operator, you make sacrifices because your business re- quires you to work nights, on weekends and even holidays, often away from your family.

Good preparation and careful consideration of what makes an owner- operator successful will help you avoid costly mistakes that can set you back or even destroy your dream.

Such a major decision affects you, your spouse and your family. Include them in your decision-making process, since your family's support will contribute to your success.

Begin with a thorough self- assessment of your skills and experience. Then list your strengths and weaknesses. This exercise will improve your self-awareness and decision making.

Use this list as your guide:
- Years of driving experience - Crisis management
- Trucking-related skills - Motivation and endurance
- Mechanical skills - Willingness to learn
- Basic business experience - Stress management
- Money management skills - Flexibility
- Basic bookkeeping - Willingness to sacrifice
- Computer skills - Familiar with Internet
- Communication style
- Other experience

The Economic Outlook for 2018

The Economic Outlook for 2018 The trucking industry's Fortunes falls and rises with the American economy. At this time, the outlook for 2018 is courteous optimistic and industry experts expect a slow but steady recovery of the economic growth experienced in 2017 will continue into next year. For 2018, a growth rate in the 3.5 - 5% range in the first quarter of 2018 is anticipated. Predicting the heavy truck market for 2018 is showing the same improvements like the 3rd quarter of 2017. There are just so many variables in the equation.

Many we can make educated guesses about. The big one though, the overall health of the economy is improving and therefore can give us a clue about 2018.

After dropping earlier in 2016 and in 2017, the Truck Tonnage Index is up 6.7%, and the long-term outlook for 2018 will see some moderate gains for the 1st and 2nd half of 2018. The reduction in sup- ply since the start of the recession means that even small improvements in tonnage will have a larger impact on the industry than in the past.

The shortage of qualified drivers, particularly in the long-haul sector, could become a long term problem after CSA 2010 is now fully implemented.

Despite the favorable outlook for 2018 with regard to capacity and revenue, carriers as well as Owner-Operators will still have to tightly control costs. A decrease in fuel prices and slightly

improved growth in freight volume may drive financially stable carriers and Owner-Operators to expand their business.

One other silver-lining is the congressional interest in energy and environmental matters.

Mandate a fuel surcharge pass-through to the person who bought the fuel.

A measure designed to protect independents and

small fleet   operators. The fuel surcharge belongs in the owners pocket, not in the brokers pocket.

At this time we can't predict the cross border capacity because President Donald Trump might renegotiate NAFTA with Canada and Mexico.

International trade and exports, particularly with Mexico and Canada, may contribute to economic growth and increase capacity because most cross- border freight moves by truck. Nevertheless, the freight markets will fall and rise according to seasonal demand as well as economic cycles. As always, the fall and pre-holiday months are busy, followed by a slowdown beginning inthe middle of December and lasting through March because there is less consumer demand. During seasons of peak demand, capacity will be tight. Since there is more demand than supply, larger carriers will be able to raise freight rates and shippers may be willing to pay premium rates to move undesirable freight and perishable goods. However, high fuel costs add to operating costs and may offset higher revenue, thereby limiting profit- ability. Nevertheless, Owner operators might have more freight to haul in 2018 and might benefit from higher rates.

The revised Hours of Service regulations which went into effect on January 4, 2004, is in effect. These rules are implemented in the new CSA 2010 regulations.

Fuel prices have not had such a devastating effect on the trucking industry as in past years.

Fuel surcharges have helped carriers deal with increased fuel costs; however, when fuel costs rise quickly, the surcharge does not always cover the in- crease. Although fuel prices went up from the national average of $2.20 in June 2017 to $2.40 in November 2017, industry experts believe fuel prices will remain at about $2.45-$2.65 in 2018.

With fuel being the #1 expense, Owner-Operators will have to continue monitoring fuel usage and plan their fuel stops to avoid having to fuel up in states where prices are high. Regional differences in fuel prices affect the Owner- Operator's profitability. The West Coast, Southwest and the Midwest have the highest regional average prices, at $2.65 to $2.85 per gallon. Fuel is more reasonable in the South and the Western Mountain regions at $2.40 to $2.65 per gallon average. Up and down the East Coast, the regional average is $2.70 per gallon.

Overall, insurance rates will remain high in 2018, particularly workers' compensation and health insurance. However, premiums for liability and cargo insurance are leveling off due to increased competition among insurers. Still, an Owner Operator can expect to pay between $7,000 and $10,000 a year for general liability insurance.

Truckers with a good safety record may see premium reductions, and there is an expectation that premiums will come down. Nevertheless, with low interest rates, it may be cheaper to borrow the money and earn a discount by paying the annual premium in one lump sum, rather than financing it through the insurance provider. To lower insurance costs, Owner Operators may raise deductibles and pay out of pocket for small claims.

Interest rates have dropped to historically low levels in recent years and are expected to remain low as the Federal Reserve continues to manage the economic expansion.

However, lower interest rates do not automatically translate into cheap financing for buying equipment. Lenders continue to limit their best deals to buyers with excellent credit because they still consider trucking a high credit risk due to the significant rate of business failures in previous years. Start- ups will have difficulty finding affordable financing, especially if they have little cash to invest.

If you're in need of financing and you're credit rating is rather low or not that good, please go to our website

www.truckingsuccess.com and consider
an SBA loan by using our business plan trucking.

The huge inventories of used trucks is even bigger now, the Owner-Operator going into business now can find a nice selection of used trucks at low prices, according to the *American Trucker* magazine.

Many dealers offer their inventories on the Internet, and prospective buyers can do comparison shopping on-line. Additionally, manufacturer-owned finance companies will offer attractive interest rates to qualified buyers to help move trucks.

The man or woman who owns and operates an 18-wheeler must have multiple talents. In addition to excel- lent driving and road skills, the successful owner-operators qualities include:

Communication skills. In the course of a day, the owner-operator may speak with dispatchers, shippers, DOT inspectors and the highway patrol. To succeed, she-he must think, speak and act like a business owner, choosing an appropriate communication style to fit the occasion.

Business skills. The owner- operator works hard and uses many resources to succeed. She-he applies sound business principles and keeps ac- curate records. She-he uses the Inter- net in the day-to-day management of the business to find loads, obtain licensing/toll information, directions, the best routes and road conditions, to ensure the load gets to the destination on time.

Solid decision-making skills.
The owner-operator knows the operating costs and uses the cost per mile calculation in order to accept good paying loads and he/she knows what route to travel.

Mechanical aptitude. Down times and expensive truck repairs eat into the profit margin. The owner- operator must have an understanding of the truck's systems and components and how they work together so (s)he can perform small repairs and deal with emergency situations on the road.

Please do not feel discouraged if you fall short on the list of skills and experience. You have one important skill: the capacity to learn. Take the time now, before you start driving your big rig, to acquire and develop the skills that will contribute to your success!

The Revised Hours-Of-Service Regulations

On January 4, 2004, the Revised Hours-Of-Service Regulations went into effect and the Federal Motor Carrier Safety Administration (FMCSA) and its state enforcement partners began enforcing the final rule on that date. Despite recent court challenges, carriers, independent truckers, and Owner Operators are required to operate under these new rules.

In April 2003, the FMCSA issued the first significant revision to the Hours-Of-Service (HOS) regulations since 1939 when the original HOS rules were prescribed for truckers.

Concerns about the effect of fatigue as a contributing factor in commercial motor vehicle (CMV) crashes and new scientific findings related to driver fatigue and sleep disorder re- search led to the new rule-making.

The FMCSA had considered re- forming the HOS regulations for some time. However, in 1995 Congress directed the FMCSA to begin rule- making on new HOS regulations that increase driver alertness and reduce fatigue-related incidents.

According to the FMCSA, the revised regulations' primary benefit is an increased opportunity for drivers to obtain needed rest and restorative sleep while reflecting the operational realities of motor carrier transportation. The new rules will improve high-way safety and help reduce the number of commercial truck crashes and related deaths and injuries.

The new rules govern drivers transporting freight in interstate commerce in a property-carrying commercial vehicle with a gross weight rating of 10,001 pounds or more, and operating vehicles transporting hazardous materials in quantities requiring vehicle placards. Rules for the record-of-duty status form, which is commonly referred to as the driver's daily log, remain un- changed for truck drivers.

The following is a summary of the new HOS rules' main points:

- <u>Daily Cycle</u>: 10 hours off and 14 hours on.
- <u>On Duty</u>: The 14 consecutive hours on duty include breaks. Local drivers may extend this to 16 hours one day a week

under certain circum- stances.

- <u>Driving Time</u>: 11 hours.
- <u>Off Duty</u>: 10 consecutive hours.
- <u>Breaks</u>: Breaks during duty time (on duty) are discretionary.
- <u>Weekly Hours</u>: If the company does not run trucks daily, a driver may not drive after 60 hours logged

   "on-duty" in 7 consecutive days. If the company runs trucks daily, a driver may not drive after 70 hours logged "on-duty" in ay period of 8 consecutive days. Time logged as "off-duty" is not counted in calculating "on-duty" time.
- <u>Weekly Break:</u> At least 34 consecutive hours (1 day 10 hours).
- <u>Restart</u>: A break of 34 consecutive hours "restarts" the weekly cycle.
- <u>Sleeper Berth:</u> Among the changes in the 2005 rules, perhaps the most significant – and most confusing – relates to the split-sleeper option. That is the option that allows a driver to split his/her required 10 consecutive hours of rest into two separate, non-consecutive breaks. Though the split-sleeper option will still be an option after October 1st for both teams and individual drivers, the requirements will change significantly – so much, in fact, that many are wondering if they should continue using the option at all.

   Under the 2003 rules, a driver could split his/her time into any combination of two breaks that added up to 10 hours, so long as the breaks were at least 2 hours long. These breaks had to be spent entirely in the berth, but they were excluded from the 14-hour limit.

Under the 2005 rules, you still need two breaks that add up to 10 hours. But, recognizing that drivers need 7 to 8 hours of continuous sleep to beat fatigue, the rules require one of the two breaks to be at least 8 continuous hours. Like the 2003 rules, this break must be spent entirely in the sleeper berth, and it will still be excluded from the 14-hour limit.

   The other break must be at least 2 hours long (this is so

that the driver gets the required 10 total hours of rest), but this break can be spent off duty, in the sleeper berth, or any combination of the two. In addition, this shorter break is always included in the 14-hour limit, no matter where it is spent (i.e., it always counts against the driver, even if it is spent in the sleeper berth). Because one of the two breaks will count against the driver's 14-hour limit, the new rules change the way you calculate available hours after a break. As under the 2003 rules, once you have completed two qualifying rest breaks that add up to 10 hours (one being at least 8 hours in a sleeper berth), you do not gain back a full 11 driving hours and 14 on-duty hours.

Rather, following the second rest break, hours available under the 11 and 14 hour rules must be recalculated from the end of the first of the two breaks.

Examples: Suppose driver Smith takes 10 hours off and starts driving. He drives for 6 hours and then decides to take a 2-hour nap. Those 2 hours will count against his 14 hour limit no matter where he takes them (off duty and/or sleeper). After his nap, he drives for his remaining 5 hours and is then at hour 13 out of 14 (6+2+5=13). To gain time back, Smith may either: Go off duty and/or in the sleeper for 10 consecutive hours; or go into the sleeper berth for only 8 hours. If he chooses to take 10 hours off, he will gain a full 11 and 14 hours. Suppose he chooses an 8 hour sleeper berth. How much driving and on-duty time does he have remaining at the end of that break? We start counting from the end of the first break (the 2 hour nap), and arrive at the following numbers:

Driving time: 11–5 hours driving after the 2 hour nap = 6 hours remaining.

Duty time: 14–5 hours spent after the 2 hour nap = 9 hours remaining.

Driver Smith starts driving again.

Suppose he uses his remaining 6 hours of driving time, has another 2 hours on duty (not driving), and wants to return to driving. At this point, he has used up his 11 hours of driving time and is at hour 13 of 14 available.

Drivers or carriers who violate the Hours-Of-Service regulations

face the following penalties:

- Drivers may be placed out of ser- vice (shut down) at roadside until the driver has accumulated enough off-duty time to be back in compliance;
- State and local enforcement officials may assess fines;

**Hours of Service of Drivers
effective July 1, 2013**

AGENCY: Federal Motor

Carrier Safety

Administration (FMCSA),

ACTION: Final rule.

SUMMARY: FMCSA revises the hours of service (HOS) regulations to limit the use of the 34- hour restart provision to once every 168 hours and to require that anyone using the 34-hour restart provision have as part of the restart two periods that include 1 a.m. to 5 a.m.

It also includes a provision that allows truckers to drive if they have had a break of at least 30 minutes, at a time of their choosing, sometime within the previous 8 hours. This rule does not include a change to the daily driving limit because the Agency is unable
to definitively demonstrate that a 10-hour limit—which it favored in the notice of proposed rulemaking (NPRM)—would have higher net benefits than an 11-hour limit. The current 11- hour limit is therefore unchanged at this time.

The 60- and 70-hour limits are also unchanged. The purpose of the rule is to limit the ability of drivers to work the maximum number of hours currently allowed, or close to the maximum, on a continuing basis to reduce the possibility of driver fatigue.

Long daily and weekly hours are associated with an increased risk of crashes and with the chronic health conditions associated with lack of sleep. These changes will affect only the small minority of drivers who regularly work the longer hours.

Compliance date: The rule changes that affect Appendix B to Part 386— Penalty Schedule; Violations and Monetary Penalties; the oilfield exemption in § 395.1(d)(2); and the definition of on-duty time in § 395.2 must be complied with on the effective date. Compliance for all the other rule changes is not required until December 18, 2017.

The Commercial Driver's License

Since April 1, 1992, the Federal Motor Carrier Safety Administration (**FMCSA**) has required drivers to possess a Commercial Driver's License (**CDL**) to operate commercial motor vehicles (**CMV**).

A driver must take the CDL test in his/her home state and cannot hold more than one commercial driver's license. The CDL replaced and invalidated previously issued chauffeur licenses.

Driving CMV's requires special skills and knowledge. Prior to implementation of the CDL Program, in a number of states and the District of Columbia, any person licensed to drive an automobile could also legally drive a tractor-trailer or a bus. Even in many of the states that did have a classified licensing system, a person was not skills tested in a representative vehicle. Many drivers were operating motor vehicles that they may not have been qualified to drive, and were able to obtain driver's licenses from more than one state and hide or spread convictions among several driving records and continue to drive.

The **Commercial Motor Vehicle Safety Act of 1986** was signed into law on October 27, 1986, with the goal to improve highway safety by ensuring that drivers of large trucks and buses are qualified to operate those vehicles and to remove unsafe and un- qualified drivers from the highways.
The Act retained the state's right to is- sue a driver's license, but established minimum national standards which states must meet when licensing CMV drivers.

> The Act corrects the situation existing prior to 1986 by making it illegal to hold more than one license and by requiring states to adopt testing and licensing standards for truck and bus drivers to check a person's ability to operate the type of vehicle (s)he plans to operate.

The Act does not require drivers to obtain a separate Federal license. It merely required states to upgrade their existing testing and licensing pro- grams, if necessary, to conform with the Federal minimum standards.

The CDL places requirements on the CMV driver, the employing motor carrier and the states. The FHWA has developed and issued standards for testing and licensing CMV drivers. Among other things, the standards require States to issue CDL's to their CMV drivers only after a driver passes knowledge and skills tests administered by the state related to the type of vehicle to be operated.
Drivers need CDL's if they are in inter- state, intrastate, or foreign commerce and drive a vehicle that meets one of the following definitions of a CMV. The Federal standard requires states to is- sue a CDL to drivers according to the following licensing classifications:

Class A — Any combination of vehicles with a GCWR of 26,001 or more pounds provided the GVWR of the vehicle(s) being towed is in excess of 10,000 pounds.

Class B — Any single vehicle with a GVWR of 26,001 or more pounds, or any such vehicle towing a vehicle not in excess of 10,000 pounds GVWR.

Class C — Any single vehicle, or combination of vehicles, that does not meet the definition of Class A or Class B, but is either designed to transport 16 or more passengers, including the driver, or is placarded for hazardous materials.

Knowledge and Skills Tests: States develop their own tests which must be at least as stringent as the Federal standards. The FMCSA has prepared model driver and examiner manuals and tests and distributed them to the states to use, if they wish.

- The general knowledge test must contain at least 30 questions.
- To pass the knowledge tests(general and endorsement), applicants must correctly answer at least 80 percent of the questions.

- To pass the skills test, applicants must successfully perform all the required skills (listed in 49 CFR 383.113). The skills test must be taken in a vehicle representative of the type of vehicle that the applicant operates or expects to operate.

Other States, employers, training facilities, governmental departments and agencies, and private institutions can serve as *third party skills testers* for the State under the following criteria:

- Tests must be the same as those given by the State.
- Examiners must meet the same qualifications as State examiners.

- States must conduct an on-site inspection at least once a year.
  At least annually, State employees must evaluate the programs by taking third party tests as if they were test applicants, or by testing a sample of drivers tested by the third party and then comparing pass/fail rates.
- The State's agreement with the third party skills tester must allow the FHWA and the State to conduct random examinations, inspections, and audits without prior notice.

The states determine the license fee, the renewal cycle, most renewalprocedures, and continue to decide the age, medical and other driver qualifications of their intrastate commercial drivers. Interstate drivers must meet the longstanding Federal driver qualifications (49 CFR 391).

All CLD's must contain the following information:

- The words "Commercial Driver's Li- cense" or "CDL."
- The driver's full name, signature, and address.
- The driver's date of birth, sex and height.
- Color photograph or digitalized image of the driver.

- The driver's state license number.
- The name of the issuing state.
- The date of issuance and the date of the expiration of the license.
- The class of vehicle that the driver is authorized to operate.
- Notation of the "air brake" restriction, if issued.
- The endorsement's) for which the driver has qualified.

States may issue learner's permits for behind-the-wheel training on public highways as long as learner's permit holders are required to be ac- companied by someone with a valid CDL appropriate for that vehicle and the learner's permits are issued for limited time periods.

CDL holders are subject to the following penalties, disqualifications and standards. Violations may result in civil or criminal penalties and the loss of the CDL.

Penalties: The Federal penalty to a driver who violates the CDL requirements is a civil penalty of up to $2,500 or, in aggravated cases, criminal penalties of up to $5,000 in fines and/or up to 90 days in prison. An employer is also subject to a penalty of up to $10,000, if (s)he knowingly uses a driver to operate a CMV without a valid CDL.

Drivers must be disqualified and lose their privilege to drive for one year for driving under the influence of a controlled substance or alcohol, or leaving the scene of an accident, or using a CMV to commit a felony.

Drivers must be disqualified and lose their privilege to drive for three years for committing any of the one- year offenses while operating a CMV that is placarded for hazardous materials.

Drivers must be disqualified and for committing a second offense of any of the one-year or three-year offenses, or using a CMV to commit a felony involving manufacturing, distributing, or dispensing controlled substances.

However, states have the option to reduce certain lifetime disqualifications to a minimum disqualification of ten years if the driver completes a driver rehabilitation program approved by the state.

If a CDL holder is disqualified from operating a CMV, the state may issue this person a license to operate non-commercial vehicles. However, states cannot issue a "conditional" or "hardship" CDL or any other type of limited driving privileges to continue driving a CMV to a disqualified driver.

Convictions for out-of-state violations are treated the same as convictions for violations that are committed in the driver's home state. The Commercial Driver's License Information System (CDLIS), to which states must be connected, ensures that convictions a driver receives outside his/her home state are transmitted to the home state so that the disqualifications can be applied.

BAC Standards: The FHWA has established **0.04 percent** as the blood alcohol concentration (BAC) level at or above which a CMV driver is considered to be driving under the influence of alcohol and subject to the disqualification sanctions in the Act.

Employer Notifications: A driver must notify his/her employer within thirty days of a conviction for any traffic violation, except parking, regardless of the nature of the violation or the type of vehicle driven at the time. An Owner-Operator under a lease contract is considered to be an employee of the carrier and must therefore report violations to the carrier.

The employer must be notified if a driver's license is suspended,

revoked, canceled, or if (s)he is disqualified from driving. The notification must be made by the end of the next business day following receipt of the suspension, revocation, cancellation, lost privilege or disqualification. from driving. Violations of this requirement may result in civil or criminal penalties. Source: www.fmcsa.gov.

CDL Manuals and Knowledge Tests may be obtained from the Motor Vehicle Division of the driver's home state. The address and telephone
numbers are listed in the blue pages under State Government in the telephone directories. Most states also provide CDL information on-line.

Most jurisdictions offer their CDL manuals in English only. However, the following jurisdictions offer the CDL manual in Spanish in some form: Arizona, California, Idaho, Michigan, Minnesota, New Jersey, New York, Texas,and D.C.

The following seventeen jurisdictions provide the CDL Knowledge Test in Spanish in some form: Arizona, California, Colorado, Delaware, Florida, Georgia, Idaho, Iowa, Minnesota, New Jersey, New York, Oregon, Texas,
Virginia, Washington, Wisconsin, and D.C.

Average time to complete the skills tests is 31 minutes for pre-trip inspections, 22 minutes for the basic control skills, and 40 minutes for the on- road driving. Source: AAMVA 1997 Commercial Driver's License Survey.

Under the PATRIOT Act of 2001, applicants for CDL's with a hazardous materials endorsement and drivers who already have a CDL with a hazmat endorsement are required to clear an FBI background check, must be finger- printed, and the endorsements must be renewed at least every five years.
Enforcement of this rule was to begin November 3, 2003, but states have asked that enforcement of this rule be postponed because all the systems needed are not yet in place. Fingerprinting is now scheduled to begin January 31, 2005.

Eventually, all truckers may be required to undergo background checks with fingerprints or some other biometric identifier. Furthermore, the Department of Homeland Security is working on a program to create a Transportation Worker Identification Credential, which is a type of universal security card which could also serve as CDL for truck drivers. The credential may be implemented after 2005.

CSA 2010

The purpose of the CSA 2010 initiative is to develop more effective and efficient methods for FMCSA, together with industry and state partners, to achieve its mission of reducing commercial motor vehicle (CMV) crashes, fatalities, and injuries.

How will your operation be impacted by CSA2010?
Because CSA2010 will audit ALL carriers and drivers and their violations, and will impose harsher fines and penalties than ever before, it will be imperative that your company understands the changes this new initiative brings to the trucking industry. CSA2010 will employ COMPASS, an electronic database for keeping records on carrier safety ratings. This system, in addition to data gathered from roadside violations, and crash reports, will enable the FMCSA to monitor carrier performance, and identify those requiring intervention.

Under CSA2010, Interventions can begin and end with a Warning Letter, or can be broadened to include off-site investigations (records audits), and finally on-site investigations. All of these can include development of corrective action plans, but may also involve fines!

Because **CSA2010 will audit ALL carriers and drivers, identifies over 1000 possible violations, and will impose harsher fines and penalties than ever be- fore**, it is imperative that your company understands the changes this new initiative brings to the trucking industry!

Unfortunately, many companies who are "satisfactory" under the current Safe Stat system WILL be found non compliant and placed in INTERVENTION status with the DOT under CSA2010. If you find yourself in this unenviable situation, you will be required to develop a measureable, results-oriented safety-training plan in order to respond to and remove yourself from intervention status. You need responsive reporting and must demonstrate to the DOT that your employees and drivers are not only going thru the safety training necessary to respond to the issues which resulted in intervention, but you should also have 3rd Party documented test results, with which to demonstrate their progress!

The CSA 2010 Operational Model has three major components:

> Measurement - CSA 2010 measures safety performance in new ways, using inspection and crash results to identify carriers whose behaviors could reasonably lead to crashes.

> Evaluation - CSA 2010 helps FMCSA and its State Partners to correct high risk behavior by contacting more carriers and drivers, with interventions tailored to their specific safety problem, as well as a new safety fitness determination methodology.

> Intervention - CSA 2010 covers the full spectrum of safety issues – from how data is collected, evaluated, and shared to how enforcement officials can intervene most effectively and efficiently to improve safety on our roads.

Safety Measurement System

Within the Comprehensive Safety Analysis (CSA 2010) Operational Model, the Safety Measurement System (SMS) quantifies the on-road safety performance of carriers and drivers to identify candidates for interventions, to determine the specific safety problems exhibited by a carrier or driver, and to monitor whether safety problems are improving or worsening. SMS replaces Safe Stat in the new Operational Model.

The carrier SMS uses a motor carrier's data from roadside inspections, including all safety-based violations, State-reported crashes, and the Federal motor carrier census to quantify performance in the following Behavior Analysis Safety Improvement Categories (BASICs).

CSA 2010 BASICs:

Unsafe Driving — Operation of commercial motor vehicles (CMVs) by drivers in a dangerous or careless manner. *Example Violations:* Speeding, reckless driving, improper lane change, and inattention. (FMCSR Parts 392 and 397)

Fatigued Driving (Hours-of-Service) — Operation of CMVs by drivers who are ill, fatigued, or in non-compliance with the Hours-of-Service (HOS) regulations. This BASIC includes violations of regulations pertaining to logbooks as they relate to HOS requirements and the management of CMV driver fatigue. *Example Violations:* HOS, logbook, and operating a CMV while ill or fatigued. (FMCSR Parts 392 and 395)

Driver Fitness — Operation of CMVs by drivers who are unfit to operate a CMV due to lack of training, experience, or medical qualifications. *Example Violations:* Failure to have a valid and appropriate commercial driver's license and being medically un- qualified to operate a CMV. (FMCSR Parts 383 and 391)

Controlled Substances/Alcohol — Operation of CMVs by drivers who are impaired due to alcohol, illegal drugs, and misuse of prescription or over- the-counter medications. *Example Violations:* Use or possession of con- trolled substances/alcohol. (FMCSR Parts 382 and 392)

Vehicle Maintenance — Failure to properly maintain a CMV. *Example Violations:* Brakes, lights, and other mechanical defects, and failure to make required repairs. (FMCSR Parts <u>393</u> and <u>396</u>)

Cargo-Related — Failure to properly prevent shifting loads, spilled or dropped cargo, overloading, and unsafe handling of hazardous materials on a CMV. *Example Violations:* Improper load securement, cargo retention, and hazardous material handling. (FMCSR Parts <u>392</u>, <u>393</u>, <u>397</u> and HM Violations)

Crash Indicator— Histories or patterns of high crash involvement, including frequency and severity. It is based on information from State-reported crashes.

A carrier's measurement for each BASIC depends on:
The number of adverse safety events (violations related to that BASIC or crashes)
The severity of violations or crashes
When the adverse safety events occurred (more recent events are weighted more heavily).

After a measurement is determined, the carrier is then placed in a peer group (e.g., other carriers with similar numbers of inspections). Percentiles from 0 to 100 are then determined by comparing the BASIC measurements of the carrier to the measurements of other carriers in the peer group. 100 indicates the worst performance.

Safety Evaluation

Safety evaluation is the process of determining how to address carriers with poor safety performance.

The Safety Measurement System (SMS) allows FMCSA to more effectively evaluate safety performance using new measures for identifying which carriers require what type of intervention using a policy-driven process called intervention selection, and

Determining which carriers should be proposed "Unfit" to operate, using a regulatory process called Safety Fitness Determination (SFD).

(An *Unfit Suspension* will prohibit a carrier from operating, based on the conclusion of a SFD. The details of Unfit Suspension will be described in the SFD Rulemaking.)

FMCSA is developing a SFD methodology, subject to ongoing rulemaking, to re- place the current system that is solely dependent on the onsite compliance review results. The SFD will expand the use of on-road performance as calculated in the SMS and include results of all investigations. It will also allow FMCSA to deter- mine safety fitness on a larger segment of the industry.

Intervention

FMCSA and State partners will use measurement results to identify carriers for CSA 2010 interventions. These interventions will offer an expanded suite of tools ranging from warning letters to comprehensive onsite investigations. These tools supplement the labor-intensive compliance review (CR) to better address the spe- cific safety problems identified.

CSA 2010 investigators will be equipped to systematically evaluate why safety problems are occurring, to recommend remedies, to encourage corrective action(s), and, where corrective action is inadequate, to invoke strong penalties. Interventions will provide carriers with the information necessary to understand their safety problems and to change unsafe behavior early on. Interventions under CSA 2010 can be broken into 3 basic categories, which are described in detail below: early contact, investigation, and follow-on.

Early Contact

<u>Warning Letter</u> - Correspondence sent to a carrier's place of business that specifically identifies a deficient BASIC(s) and outlines possible consequences of continued safety problems. The warning letter provides instructions for accessing carrier safety data and measurement as well as a point of contact.

Carrier Access to Safety Data and Measurement - Carriers have access to their measurement results (BASICs scores), as well as the inspection reports and violations that went into those results. With this information, carriers can chart a course of self-improvement. Carriers can also monitor this data for accuracy and challenge it as necessary through FMCSA's Data Qs system: https://dataqs.fmcsa.dot.gov/login.asp.

Targeted Roadside Inspection - CSA 2010 provides roadside inspectors with data that identifies a carrier's specific safety problems, by BASIC, based on the new measurement system. Targeted roadside inspections occur at permanent and temporary roadside inspection locations where connectivity to the SMS information is available. As Commercial Vehicle Information Systems and Networks (CVISN) technologies evolve they will be incorporated into the roadside inspections.

Investigation

Offsite Investigation - A carrier is required to submit documents to FMCSA or a State Partner. These documents are used to evaluate the safety

problems identified through the SMS and to determine their root causes. Types of documents re- quested may include third party documents such as toll receipts, border crossing records, or drug testing records. The goal is to identify issues responsible for poor safety performance. If the carrier does not submit requested documents they may be subject to an onsite investigation or to subpoena records (see below).

Onsite Investigation - Focused - The purpose of this intervention is to evaluate the safety problems identified through the SMS and their root causes. An onsite focused investigation may be selected when deficiencies in two or less BASICs exist. Onsite "focused" investigations target specific problem areas (for example, maintenance records), while onsite "comprehensive" investigations address all asects of the carrier's operation.

Onsite Investigation - Comprehensive - This intervention is similar to a CR and takes place at the carrier's place of business. It is used when the carrier exhibits broad and complex safety problems through continually deficient BASICs, worsening multiple BASICs (three or more), or a fatal crash or complaint.

Follow-on

Cooperative Safety Plan (CSP) - Implemented by the carrier, this safety improvement plan is voluntary. The carrier and FMCSA collaboratively create a plan, based on a standard template, to address the underlying problems resulting from the car- rier's substandard safety performance.

Notice of Violation (NOV) - The NOV is a formal notice of safety deficiencies that requires a response from the carrier. It is used when the regulatory violations dis- covered are severe enough to warrant formal action but not a civil penalty (fine). It is also used in cases where the violation is immediately correctable and the level of, or desire for, cooperation is high. To avoid further intervention, including fines, the carrier must provide evidence of corrective action or initiate a successful challenge to the violation.

Notice of Claim (NOC) - A NOC is issued in cases where the regulatory violations are severe enough to warrant assessment and issuance of civil penalties.

Operations Out-of-Service Order (OOS) - An order requiring the carrier to cease all motor vehicle operations.

Choosing A Legal Business Structure

Sole proprietorships, partner- ships, corporations, and limited liability companies are the most common legal structures for small businesses. No one legal structure is right for all small businesses. Whether starting the business as a sole proprietor or choosing one of the more complicated organizational structures depends on several factors.

A **sole proprietorship** is the basic and simple form of a business
organization and has no existence apart from the owner. The spouse can be an informal owner of your sole proprietor- ship.
The business liabilities are also the owner's liabilities. Ownership (proprietary) interest ends when the owner dies.
The owner undertakes the risks of business to the extent of all of his/ her assets. There is no differentiation between the business and the owner's private assets. The owner is responsible for loss, gain or damage.
The owner is responsible for estimated tax payments on a quarterly basis to the IRS, if the estimated tax payment is more than $500. Sole
proprietors pay taxes on business income on their personal

tax returns.

A **partnership** is the relationship existing between two or more persons who join together to carry on a trade or business. A business with more than one person that is not incorporated or organized as an LLC is a partnership by default.

The term partnership includes a syndicate, group, pool, joint venture, or other unincorporated organizations that carries on a business and is not classified as a trust, estate or corporation.

Each person joining the partner- ship contributes money, property, labor or skill and expects to share in the profits and losses of the business.

A partnership agreement or added modifications may be oral or written. If there is an oral agreement, witnesses should be present or it should be recorded on tape.

Generally, a partner's share of income, gain, loss, deductions, or credits is determined by the partnership agreement. The liabilities of a partnership are determined by the number of shares (s)he acquires when signing the agreement.

However, the liability is every partner's responsibility including his personal as- sets depending on the percentage (s)he owns in a partnership.
A partnership is not a taxable entity, and each partner is responsible for paying estimated taxes and filing tax returns.

A **corporation** is the most important form to organize a business be- cause it comes into existence by an act of the state and therefore is a legal entity. It has a definite existence through legal papers filed with the State, generally the Secretary of State or the Corporation Commission.

A corporation has perpetual existence as long as it is compliant with annual filing requirements of the Secretary of State or the Corporation Com- mission.

Registration of a corporate name shall contain the word "corporation," "company," or "incorporated," or shall contain an abbreviation of one of such words.

The corporate name should not be the same as, or deceptively similar to, the name of any domestic corporation existing under the law of the same state in which the new corporation will be registered.

A corporation provides protection from personal liability for business debts. The liability of its owners is limited to their investments, and their per- son estates are not liable for the obligations of the corporation. However, failure to comply with and follow corporate formalities or keep adequate records can result in the loss of the limited liability status.

Corporations consist of share- holders, who are the owners of the business. A minimum of two persons is required to create a corporation. A board of directors, which is elected by the shareholders, manages the business.

S Corporations: Certain corporations can choose to qualify underSubchapter S of the Internal RevenueCode to avoid the imposition of income taxes at the corporate level while retaining all the advantages of a corporation. Income from an S Corporation is taxed as personal income on Schedule E (Form 1040).

A corporation must meet these requirements to qualify for a
S Corporation status:

- Be a domestic corporation.
- Not be a member of an affiliated group of corporations.
- Have only one class of stock. Not all shareholders need to

have the same voting rights.

- Have 35 or fewer shareholders.

- No shareholder of the corporation can be a non-resident alien.
- Shareholders must be individuals, estates or certain trusts.
- Corporations, partnerships and non- qualifying trusts cannot be share- holders.

Limited Liabilities Companies (LLC) combine some of the best
attributes of corporations and partnerships, including limited personal liability and one level of taxation.

LLC owners report business in- come and losses on their personal in- come tax returns, thus avoiding double taxation.

Articles of organization must include the name of the LLC, the address of the registered office, the name of a statutory agent, a dissolution date, and information about management.

Filing requirements and fees are similar to those of a corporation.

- **Each form of business has ad- vantages and disadvantages. The independent truck-owner operator should carefully study the options and make a decision based on his or her personal circumstances and applicable state and tax laws. An accountant or**
- **Once the owner-operator has selected a form of business organization, (s)he must make sure that (s)he understands the specifics of that structure and follows the requirements to stay compliant with federal, state, local and tax laws.**

Buying Your Truck

Starting a business requires a significant capital investment. And few start-ups have succeeded on a shoe-string budget. This is especially true for the capital-intensive transportation industry. The start-up Owner-Operator needs cash for the down payment on a truck, the registration, permits, and insurance as well as for the day-to–day operation of the truck until revenue starts flowing in.

Buying that first truck is an emotional experience, and the decision will have long-term implications. Therefore, you must carefully research the marketand choose well-maintained, easy-to-handle and reliable equipment.

Before selecting a truck, the Owner-Operator needs to establish business connections where (s)he can get loads. That means talking directly to manufacturers and businesses, transportation brokers, and/or obtaining information from carriers about their lease-on programs, and checking references. Owner Operators can also utilize a consulting service that will help and teach Owner Operator's how to establish business relationships and how to find good paying loads. TruckingSuccess.com offers such a consulting service for a modest fee.
To sign up for this service, please call (602) 864-8056

Although you may dream of a fancy, shiny new truck, a good quality used truck with a modest monthly payment will make more sense for the Owner-Operator who has to gain industry experience. Most Owner- Operators prefer long-nose trucks, but for the beginner cab-overs offer better value for the money, because they are considerably cheaper than conventional trucks.

A buyer can choose from a huge selection of pre-owned trucks, which are offered through Internet auctions, used truck sale magazines, dealerships, private parties, and manufacturers.
For a listing of the largest used truck locator, visit www.putrucks.com.

Also consider such factors as fuel efficiency and cab comfort because you spend most of your day driving.
Fuel costs make up a significant part of the operating expenses, and a fuel efficient truck can greatly improve the business's bottom line.

An Owner-Operator will need between $5,000 to $10,000 just for the cost associated with the purchaseof a good used truck in addition to financing the rest of the truck's purchase price.

Used truck prices range from:
$10,000 to over $50,000, but a good four– to five-year-old Cab-over should sell for approximately $20,000, with a down payment of $4,000 to $5,000.
The finance company will require a down payment of 10 to 20 percent, depending on the buyer's credit rating, and may also require a cosigner. Interest rates generally are higher than regular vehicle loans be- cause only a few companies specialize in truck financing.

Additional expenditures include the registration fee (license plate) and operating permits, as well as insurance premiums. The Owner-Operator will need several types of coverage. Department of Transportation regulations require liability coverage, however,other coverage, such as physical dam- age or workers' compensation, may be necessary to comply with state regulations or to meet shipper requirements. Insurance rates have significantly in- creased due to losses associated with the terrorist attacks. Most Owner- Operators make a down-payment and finance the annual premium, making monthly payments. About 15 insurance companies specialize in truck insurance, and most require three monthly premiums upfront, which amounts to several thousand dollars, and nine monthly payments.

The Owner-Operator will need financial resources to cover several weeks of operating expenses until revenue starts flowing in.

Some brokers may pay right away when you present documents that you have delivered the load, but most brokers and lease-on carriers will make weekly or biweekly disbursements.

Additionally, you will incur smaller expenditures for a CB radio, having your business name and DOT number painted on your truck, buying a ELD and office supplies, as well as supplies and items you will need for the sleeper.

Selecting a good used truck

A lot of equipment is available on the used truck market, but as the industry continues to struggle with high fuel costs, it is important to select aero- dynamic and fuel-efficient equipment to reduce operating costs.

The Used Truck Association (UTA) has released a set of guidelines for "industry standard" trade terms and conditions. These are used to establish the condition of a used truck, asagreed by the buyer and seller. The UTA *Trade Terms & Conditions* covers

engines, drive-trains,
brakes, tires, frames, cabs, sleepers, and bodies. It
also takes into consideration de- identification, safety
inspections and fleet trades. A free copy is available
at www.uta.org. Source: Transportation Equipment
News.

Visit the truck dealerships in your area and check the
equipment they have in stock. You will hopefully find several trucks
that meet your specifications. When you talk to a salesperson, ask
questions and take notes. You should have prepared a list of items
you need to know to help you make a purchase decision. Some of
the questions you need to ask should include:

- How many miles are on the chassis?
- How many miles are on the major components such as the
  engine, transmission, differentials, turbo charger, power
  steering, and air- conditioning system?
- Is the truck or certain components still under factory
  /manufacturer warranty?
- Does the dealership offer a warranty?
- Are used-equipment warranties available for you to
  purchase?

Who performed the truck **maintenance and where?**
- Are maintenance records available?
- For what type of service was the truck used
  for?
- How many previous owners?
- In what climate was the truck operated?
- Does the truck have all original components?
- If not, which components have been replaced and why?
- Has the engine been overhauled?
- Has the truck been in an accident or collision?

Ask additional questions and demand explanations or
clarifications if you do not understand what the sales person tells

you. You need to make sure that you learn as much as possible about the truck that you want to purchase, and an honest dealer will respect that. Also resist any pressure to close the deal until you have all the answers and explanations you need to make your final decision. Keep in mind that you invest a great deal of money in this truck and your success as an Owner-Operator will in part depend on your ability to select a well- maintained used truck whose major components will perform well for you.

Also perform a close and careful visual inspection. Start by walking around the vehicle, looking for physical damage such as body work, bent wheels, broken springs, frayed air lines, chipped or cracked lines, metal fatigue, welding marks, and anything unusual.

Then check the engine. Tilt the cab or hood and check the outer surface for leaks. Also look for signs of leakage on the side of the engine block just below the cylinder head. Ask for an explanation if it appears as if the engine was steam cleaned.

Next, pull out the oil dipstick and check for water beads. If you find water on the dipstick, it may indicate a sealing problem. Again, ask for an explanation. Then start the engine and let it idle for about fifteen minutes and check for leaks again. Ask for a test drive and take the salesperson with you to answer any questions you may have. The test drive may reveal trouble spots or problems that would otherwise hide by only idling the engine. While you drive the truck, also check for smoke. Heavy black smoke may indicate injector, pump or engine breathing problems.

The next major component to check is the transmission. If the truck has a transmission temperature gauge, watch it. The normal transmission temperature should be 200 degrees Fahrenheit or below. You should also check the transmission and rear axles for leaks. Then carefully check for cracks on the frame and make sure no welding was done at the frame rails.

Congratulations if you found the perfect truck with which to begin yourtrucking business. If not, do not hesitate to walk away from a bad deal and start searching again.

Maintenance and Repair

Getting your truck serviced regularly and keeping it well maintained will help prevent costly repairs and breakdowns on the road as well as extends the lifespan of your equipment.

Your truck dealership will per- form some of the service work, if your truck is covered by a manufacturer's warranty or if you purchased a used truck warranty. However, dealerships usually charge higher prices than independently owned shops.

Many service stations at truck stops offer specials for basic services. You may find it more convenient and time efficient to get routine maintenance such as oil changes done at truck stops while you are on the road.

As an alternative, find a small and independently owned repair shop where you can develop a personal relationship with the owner and mechanics. This will help you get your truck repaired or serviced without long waiting periods, maybe even on weekends, so you can get back on the road without delay. This will reduce unproductive downtime.

Regular preventive maintenance and inspections will help you spot minor problems early and you can repair them before they turn into major problems. The truck is your business and you have to keep it in excellent operating condition in order to run a safe and profitable business.

Make the daily pre-trip inspection part of your preventive maintenance routine. During the daily inspection, check a list of items on the truck and trailer's in— and outside. Follow the same daily routine, so nothing gets missed or overlooked. If you are leased to a carrier, you may be required to follow a specific inspection pattern. Otherwise, use this outline:

- Overview of the entire tractor- trailer:
- Engine compartment—check fluid levels, fluid leaks, belts, battery,   wiring, and compressor.
- Inside the cab start the engine, check gauges and controls, check the windshield and function of wipers and washer, windows and mirrors, emergency equipment, test air brake, check steering, the log book.
- Check lights high and low beams, four-way flashers.
- Walk around—check tires, wheels, turn signals, couplings, fifth wheel, landing gear, brakes, axles, sliders, spare tire, fuel

tanks, exhaust system, cargo-securement, suspension.
- Perform brake check.
- Check signal lights.

Federal law requires a driver to complete an inspection report after each day. Any defects noted must be repaired. The mechanic performing the repairs must sign the report andcertify that repairs have been made. The inspection report serves as a re-minder of items to check after eachday of driving. It also provides proof of inspection and the repairs.

The Department of Transportation (DOT) also conducts roadside inspections, and officers can legally stop a truck at any time. This officer may be a federal or state department of transportation (DOT) employee, a high- way patrol officer, weigh master, or other government official.

This inspection can take place along a roadside, at a rest area, a scale, or at a port of entry station. If your truck fails the inspection, the officer can declare the truck "out of service." This means you cannot drive your vehicle until the re- pairs are made and a re-inspection takes place. An inspection takes about thirty minutes. When your truck passes the inspection, you will receive a sticker that is valid for three months.

A preventive maintenance pro- gram consists of the above outlined daily routine check and the regular service check. These service checks include replacing parts before they wear out or fail.

Service checks have three levels. Items covered at the basic service Level A include grease jobs, brake adjustments, check of fluid levels, tread depth of tires, and leaks. Level B includes all the work done for Level A plus changing the oil and the oil and fuel filter. Level C service includes engine tuning, brake jobs, and replacing or rebuilding worn and failing parts.
Climatic or seasonal weather conditions require specific preventive maintenance. When you operate in hot weather

conditions such as in the South- western U.S., you need to check the condition of coolant hoses and the and the tightness of the water pump and fan belts regularly. In cold weather conditions, regularly check the antifreeze level, and the heaters and defrosters.

Operating Authority

The **Federal Highway Administration (FHA)** and its agencies is the regulatory authority for the trucking industry. A motor carrier must obtain an interstate operating authority from FHA before the carrier can engage in interstate trucking.

The truly independent trucker prefers to have his/her own operating authority; however, the start-up Owner- Operator may choose to use another carrier's authority by leasing on to that carrier.

If you are a relatively inexperienced Owner-Operator, leasing on will allow you to get hands-on industry experience and a regular paycheck while the carrier handles the details of pro-viding the operating permits, loads, a trailer, fuel cards, etc.

Carrier leases are governed by federal laws. You can locate the applicable statutes in Title 49 of the United States Code, 49 CFR Part 376, Lease and Interchange of Vehicles. Onlinesearch for "49CR376" at www.access.gpo.gov/nara/cfr.index.html. And recently a U.S. appeals court has ruledthat Owner-Operators have the right to sue carriers that do not comply with federal leasing regulations. Many trucking companies now offer lease programs for owner operators as well as lease-purchase programs. Most programs sound very good, but please be aware of unscrupulous carriers.
They can cost you thousands of dollars and put you out of business.

If you consider leasing on, obtain copies of leases from several carriers that interest you and study them carefully. If a carrier does not want to provide you with a copy for your review, pass on it. Truth-in-leasing laws entitle you to a copy of the lease before you sign it. Make sure you understand the implications before you sign a lease, and never pick up a load before you read the lease.

Provisions a lease should contain and specify:

- It must clearly detail the responsibility of the carrier and the owner- operator with respect to cost such as fuel, fuel taxes, deadheading, tolls and permits, base plates and licenses, and what happens to any unused portions of these items.
- It must clearly specify who is responsible for loading and unloading, and who pays for lumping.
- The carrier must pay you for loads within 15 days of submission of the paperwork.
- If you get paid on a percentage basis, you are entitled to a copy of a rated freight bill before or when you get paid for the load.
- Only items specified in the lease can be deducted from the settlement.
- The lease must state the amount of the escrow fund and to which items it may beapplied. The carrier must pro- vide an accounting of the escrow fund, either on the settlement form or once a month on a separate form. The lease must give the owner-operator the right to ask for an account of the fund on demand. And while the carrier controls the fund, it must pay interest. All deductions from the escrow fund must be specified in the lease, and a final account of the fund must be pro- vided and the balance be paid no later than 45 days from the owner operator's last day with the carrier.

- Terminate your lease in writing and within any specified termination period.

The carrier and you must sign an original and two copies of the lease. The carrier keeps the original and you must keep one copy in your truck. File the other copy with your business documents.

Never sign a lease under pressure and in haste. Question everything you do not understand, because once your signature is on that document, it is a legally binding contract. Avoid leases for specific periods of time such as three months or a year. Instead, opt for a month- to-month lease so you can give notice and terminate your lease within a reasonable time should things not work out. Always pay for your own base plate and fuel tax, because many carriers charge a flat rate and fail to give an accounting and refund of over-payments. Avoid unknown carriers and check an incorporated carrier's status with the Corporation Commission.

If the information on file with Corporation Commission is scant, avoid the carrier.
Ask for references and talk to other Owner-Operators that are leased on to the company with which you are negotiating. If you get negative feed- back, reconsider your choice.
And always ask to see the equipment you're signing on to. Don't sign anything before you can inspect what you're getting.

The once complicated process of obtaining your own interstate operating authority has been simplified and you can even apply online.
Why should you get your own authority? The answer is simple: it will give you more independence to make decisions how to run your operation.
You can find your own loads and negotiate the freight rates, or you can work with reputable brokers to find loads for you.
You will need to follow these steps to get your authority:
- Obtain an **application** for Motor Property Carrier & Broker Authority from the Federal Motor Carrier Safety Administration

(FMCSA), either by mail or online at http:// diy.dot.gov. The website also includes information about filing requirements.

- Obtain **liability insurance**. Federal regulations require all for-hire carriers to have liability insurance. The minimum coverage is $750,000, ifyou do not haul hazardous materials. Hazmat carriers must have $1 million to $5 million minimum coverage, depending on what they haul. In addition, common carriers need a minimum of $100,000 in cargo insurance. Your insurance company or agent must send the needed forms to FMCSA. They must be submitted within 90 days of application.

- You need a **legal process agent** for each state in which you operate. If there are legal proceedings against you, the legal process agent is the person who will officially receive any papers served. Your insurance company may provide this service to you. If not, companies that offer compliance services are also legal process agents.
- Obtain **DOT number** by submitting a Motor Carrier Identification Report (Form MCS-150) and obtain a DOT number from FMCSA. You must do this before you begin operations, and your DOT number along with your company name must appear on your vehicle(s).

   The UCR (Unified Carrier Registration) is a program that replaced the (SSRS) Single State Registration System. The UCR Program requires individuals and companies that operate commercial motor vehicles in interstate or international commerce to register their business with a participating state and pay an annual fee based on the size of their fleet. This includes ALL carriers and truck owners, private, exempt, or for hire. Kentucky, New Mexico, New York, and Oregon still require additional tax credentials.

- Obtain **IFTA license** from your base state. (Please see Registration section for details about UCR, IRP and IFTA.)

Keeping Business Records

When you start your own trucking business, you are also responsible for keeping accurate records, making tax payments and filing tax returns.

Except in a few cases, the law does not require any special kind of records. You may choose any system that is best suited for your business and that clearly shows your income. An accountant can help you decide which system to use. If you do not have an accountant yet, hire a trustworthy accountant who has knowledge of the trucking industry.

The accountant can help you set up a record and bookkeeping system., and will also prepare your tax returns. However, you can save money by doing most of the bookkeeping tasks yourself. If you use a computer in your business, a basic bookkeeping program can assist you in this task. If you have no bookkeeping experience, your accountant or a bookkeeping service can keep your books for you, but it will cost you money. Your accountant can also prepare monthly, quarterly, and year-end financial statements, so you can measure the progress of your business. You should also keep personal and business finances separate. Therefore, you should open a business checking account.

Reasons to Keep Records:
- Business owners must keep records.
- Good records help monitor the progress of your business and help you determine what changes you mustmake. Good records increase the likelihood of your success.
- Good records help prepare accurate financial statements, which include income (profit and loss) statements and balance sheets. These statements can help you in dealing with your bank or creditors.
- Good records identify the source of receipts. You receive

money or property from various sources and need to identify and separate business and non-business receipts and taxable and non-taxable income.
- Good records help you keep track of deductible expense.
- Good records help in the preparation of your tax return.

You must keep your business re- cords available at all times for inspection by the Internal Revenue Service (IRS). If the IRS conducts an audit and examines any of your tax returns, you may be asked to explain the items re- ported. A complete set of records will speed up the examination and may avoid additional taxation.

Kinds of Records to Keep:
- The law does not require any special kind of records. You may choose any system suited to yourbusiness that clearly shows your income.
- The business you are in affects the type of records you need to keep for federal and state tax purposes. You should set up your books using an accounting system that clearly shows your income for your tax year.
- The books must show your gross in- come as well as your deductions and credits. In addition, you must keep supporting documents. Purchases, sales, payroll, and other transactions you have in your business will generate supporting documents such as invoices and receipts.
- These documents contain the information you need to record in your books. It is important to keep these documents in an orderly fashion and in a safe place.

How Long to Keep Records:
- You must keep your records for as long as they may be needed for the administration of any provision of the Internal Revenue Code. Generally, this means you must keep records that support an item of income or deduction on a return until the period of limitations for that re- turn runs out.
- The period of limitations is the period of time in which you can amend your return to claim a credit or re- fund. It is

three years after the date your return is due or filed and two years after the date the tax is paid. The IRS has three years from the date you file your return to assess any additional tax. If someone files a fraudulent return or no returns at all, the IRS has a muchlonger period of time to assess additional taxes.

- If you have employees, you must keep all employment tax records for at least four years after the date the tax becomes due or is paid, whichever is later.

Accounting Periods: Every tax payer, business or individual, must figure taxable income and file a tax re- turn on the basis of an annual accounting period.

Your "tax year" is the annual ac- counting period you use for keeping your records and reporting of your in- come and expenses. The accounting periods you can use are **(1) a calendar year or (2) a fiscal year.** If your tax year begins on January 1 and ends on December 31, the due date for filing your tax return is April 15, following the tax year. The due date for corporate tax returns is March 15, following the tax year.

A fiscal tax year consists of twelve consecutive months ending on the last day of any month except December. The due date for filing your tax return is 2.5 months after your fiscal year ended. For example, the fiscal year runs from July 1 to June 30, you file your tax return on or before September 15.

Accounting Methods: Generally, you may use any of the following methods:

- Cash method,
- Accrual method,
  Special methods of accounting for certain items of income and expenses, and
- Combination (hybrid) method using elements of two or more of the above.

Most individuals and many small businesses with no inventories use the **Cash Method** of accounting. This method cannot be used by (1) corporations (other than S corp.), (2) partner ships having a corporation (other than an S corp.) as a partner, and (3) tax shelters. With this method, you include in your gross income all items of income you actually or constructively receive during the year and you must deduct expenses in the tax year in which you actually pay them.

- Under an **Accrual Method** of ac- counting, income generally is reported in the year earned, and expenses are deducted or capitalized in the year incurred. The purpose of this accounting method is to match your income and expenses in the correct year.
- **Special Methods** of accounting are used for certain items of income or expenses such as depreciation, amortization and depletion, deduction for bad debts, and installment sales.

Combination method: Generally, you may use any combination of cash, accrual, and special methods of accounting if the combination clearly shows income and you use it consistently. However, restrictions apply.

Change in Accounting Method.

When you first file your return, youmay choose any permitted accounting method. However, the method you choose must be used consistently from year to year and clearly show your in- come. If you want to change your ac- counting method after your first return is filed, you must first get consent from the IRS.

Please note: *The information presented in this section is of a general and informative nature and does not constitute tax or legal advice.*

Setting Up Your Own Record Keeping System. In order to comply with the requirements for keeping accurate records as discussed above, you need to device your own record keeping system. Most of your financial transactions will be in cash, check or credit cards and will take place while you are out on the road conducting your business. To keep track of your expenses on the road, always obtain a receipt when you buy something or pay for service. Carry a receipt book with you to record payment of lumper fees, etc. Make sure all receipts are dated, show a (business) name, and the purpose of the purchase or payment.

Use your business checks to pay for expenses such as truck payments, repairs, supplies, insurance premium payments, and license or permit fees. Match the canceled checks with the corresponding invoices or bills and you will have an accurate receipt.

When you travel, keep all your receipts in a trip envelope. Then collect all your receipts, invoices and canceled checks from your trip envelopes and file them in a separate file in chronological order. When you do your monthly bookkeeping, all you have to do is separate them by type of expenses.

You also must keep track of your Accounts Payable, that is money owed to you. When you receive a payment, attach the check stub to the corresponding invoice and file it until you do your monthly bookkeeping.

Accurate records will reflect the financial state of your business and tell you if you are making or losing money. You can also make comparisons from month to month or year to year, to determine if your business is growing and remains stagnant. Additionally, accurate records will help ensure the tax assessment on you income is fair.

The following documents can as- sist you to keep accurate records, organize your business, save you money, and make your business profitable:

- **Trip report** — recaps your travel routes and how many miles you have driven.
- **Expense report** — summarizes your trip expenses for meals, motels, showers, tolls, fuel, etc.

- **Bank statements** — shows the activity of your business bank account.
- **Settlement sheet** — summarizes your payment for the load and deductions for commission, advances (comp checks), etc.
- **Cost-Per-Mile-Calculation** —shows how much it costs you to drive a mile and will help you determine what loads to accept or reject.

    Equipment records: Besides your financial records, you also have to keep accurate records for your equipment. You have to maintain the following documentation:

- The identification of your vehicle, make, serial number, year, and tire size.
- A schedule of that shows the typeand due date of the various inspections and maintenance operations that have to be performed.
- Records of actual inspection, repair or maintenance, and date and type.
- Proof that lubrications were performed.

    You must maintain these records for at least one full year. If you sell your truck, you must keep these records for at least another six months.

    Establishing a routine will help you stay organized. Before you go on a trip, review your last inspection re- port and verify that all the noted re- pairs have been completed and that your truck is in proper operating condition.

When you come back from a trip, or at the end of your work day, complete a written vehicle inspection report, noting any repairs or work that needs to be performed so you can go back on the road with a safe vehicle that meets all requirements. You must keep a copy of the last vehicle report in the truck and every motor carrier must keep the original for at least three months.

    Your trucking business must also have a safety rating from the United States Department of Transportation (DOT). The Motor

Carrier Safety Act of 1984 requires the Secretary of Transportation to determine the safety fitness of all motor carriers operating in interstate or foreign commerce.

You may obtain information about the safety ratings from the DOT's Public Information Office in Washington, DC, phone (202) 366- 5580, or your state's DOT office.

Accounts Payable: You will have to make regular monthly pay- ments such as truck payments and insurance in addition to other bills you may receive. These billings are called "Accounts Payable."

Accounts Receivable: Every time you complete delivery of a load, money is owed to you. Your

outstanding (unpaid) settlement checks are called "Accounts Receivable."

You have to keep track of these accounts because you need your in- come to pay your expenses. If you do not get paid on time, you cannot pay your bills on time. A simple method to maintain an overview of your financial obligations is using a monthly calendar where you record the individual amounts on their due dates.

Whenever you receive or make a payment, simply mark it off as shown on the sample calendar.

January 1, 2018 Day Off	January 2, 2018 Settle- ment	January 3, 2018 Truck payment
January 4, 2018	January 5, 2018 Insurance	January 6, 2018 Tire bill

Cost-Per-Mile Calculation

You need to know two factors: (1) your operating expenses for a specific time period (a month, a calendar quarter, or a year) and (2) the miles driven in the corresponding time period.

For example if your quarterly operating expenses amount to $15,205.00 and you have driven 22,194 miles in that quarter, your cost per mile is 69 cents. You can obtain these numbers from your monthly or quarterly financial statements. Why is it important to know your cost-per-mile factor? Because it allows you to quickly determine the profitability of a load.

Now that you have identified the operating cost, you start to think about ways to lower your cost and increase your profit margin. Keep in mind, if you have operated your truck only for a short time, the cost-per-mile factor may be misleading, because you do not yet have comparable historical data from previous years.

However, as a responsible business manager you should compare your cost-per-mile factor from month to month to determine how your business progresses.

Steps you can take to reduce operating expenses include:

- slow down and drive 60 miles per hour;
- use high quality, synthetic motor oil, and
- practice preventive maintenance.

You can realize savings of thousand dollars a year just by driving your truck at 60 mph. Engine manufacturers such as Volvo say, slowing down will (1) reduce fuel consumption, (2) reduce tire wear by as much as one fifth, and (3) extends the truck engine's life- cycle, thus delaying the need for an engine overhaul. Study the following examples to see the dramatic difference: Assuming you drive **125,000** miles at **70 mph** with a fuel efficiency of **5.5** miles per gallon, your truck consumes **22,727** gallons of fuel. Assuming you drive **125,000** miles a year at **60** mph with a fuel efficiency of **7** miles per gallon, your truck consumes **17,857** gallons of fuel. Slowing down will save **4,870** gallons of fuel, or **$12,905.50** at $2.65 per gallon of fuel.

Tire expenses constitute a significant part of your business budget and you have to replace worn tires to remain compliant with the law. You can extend the lifespan of your tires by driving carefully, avoiding speeding and proper tire maintenance.

Driving your truck at 60 mph can reduce tire wear by 20 percent. If your tire budget is $5,000 a year, you can save $1,000 a year by driving at 60 mph instead of 70 mph.

Three preventable problems cause premature tire wear. (1) **Improper inflation pressure** causes tires to run much hotter. An under-inflated tire will squirm and scrub the road surface much more than a properly inflated tire. The heat and friction combine to destroy a tire quickly. Therefore, keep the tires properly inflated.

Tire/Wheel Imbalance will cause a tire to hop off the road surface once for each revolution. With a tire turning between 400 and 600 rpm depending at speed, an out-of-balance steer tire hops off the road surface eight times a second, accumulating thousands of extra tire/road impacts a day. The best time to perform an on-vehicle balance check is at oil change time. (3) **Misalignment of any axle** causes tires to scuff along the road. If you run an average of 600 miles per day, the scuff results in rapid tire wear. To reduce tire wear, all rear axles must be aligned "straight ahead" within 1/32nd inch, all rear axles must be parallel within 1.32nd inch, and the steer axle toe-in must be accurate within 1/32nd inch.

A few basic maintenance procedures can increase tire mileage at least 30 percent. A new high quality steer tire costs approximately $425 and has a lifespan of 85,000 to 100,000 miles.

By implementing three maintenance steps, you can increase the life- span of your steer tires by 25,500 to 30,000 miles:
- check tire pressure frequently;
- make wheel balance a preventive maintenance procedure; and
- check alignment of all axles on your truck, including trailer, three timesper year.

Registration & Taxes

Before you can legally operate your big rig in interstate commerce, you must:
- file Form 2290, Heavy Vehicle Use Tax, with the IRS,
- register the truck with IRP,
- register the truck with SSR, and
- register with IFTA.

Vehicle Registration. The Inter- modal Surface Transportation Act of 1991 created the **International Registration Plan (IRP)**, which is a stream- lined system for truck registration and fuel tax reporting. Every state is a member of IRP, and your base (home) state's motor vehicle division is responsible for the licensing and registration of motor carriers under the IRP and the International Fuel Tax Agreement (IFTA).

Although you must register in every state you operate your truck, and each state collects vehicle registration fees and various taxes, under IRP you fill out one form indicating the states you will drive through and pay the registration fee to your base state. Only one license plate and one cab card is issued for each vehicle registered under IRP. The vehicle is known as an apportioned vehicle. Your cab card lists the states where your vehicle is apportioned. If you have to drive through a state where your truck is not registered, you can obtain a temporary registration.

In addition to IRP, you also need **Single State Registration System (SSRS)**, which is now replaced by **UCR**.

What is the UCR?
The UCR (Unified Carrier Registration) is a program that replaced the (SSRS) Single State Registration System. The UCR Program requires individuals and companies that operate commercial motor vehicles in interstate or international

commerce to register their business with a participating state and pay an annual fee based on the size of their fleet. This includes ALL carriers and truck owners – private, exempt, or for hire. Brokers, freight forwarders and leasing companies are also required to register and pay a fee unless they also operate as a motor carrier.

Like SSRS, fees collected from the UCR system will be used by the states to support its safety programs and US- DOT officer training. Unlike SSRS, the UCR system increases the number of fee-eligible transportation companies and its owned equipment, but lowers the fee per company.

Kentucky, New Mexico, New York, and Oregon still require additional tax credentials.

Fuel & Road Taxes

The Heavy Duty Road Tax: Due on July 1st every year. If you fail to pay the tax on time, the IRS will assess penalties and late fees.

After the IRS has processed your Form 2290, you will receive a stamped copy for your records. Also keep the canceled check as proof of payment with your records.

The IRS provides Form 2290, Heavy Vehicle Use Tax Return, and it is self-explanatory. However, if you prefer, your accountant or a permit service can file the form for you.

The International Fuel Tax Agreement (IFTA) regulates the ad- ministration of road and fuel taxes among member jurisdictions. The purpose of **IFTA** is to establish and maintain the concept of one fuel use license and administering base jurisdiction for each licensee. A qualified motor vehicle is a motor vehicle used, designed, or maintained for transportation of persons or property and:

- Having two axles and a gross vehicle weight or registered gross vehicle weight exceeding 26,000 pounds; or
- Having three or more axles regardless of weight; or

  is used in combination, when such combination exceeds 26,000 pounds. Source: Arizona Motor Carrier Services.

The Owner-Operator (licensee) receives one fuel tax license, which is issued by the base state and authorizes travel in all IFTA jurisdictions. The IFTA license is valid for a calendar year, from January 1 to December 31, requiring annual renewals. You (the licensee) must file quarterly fuel tax returns reporting all miles accumulated by your truck in each jurisdiction (member state) to your base (home) state. The report must show all miles traveled and fuel purchased and consumed in each IFTA jurisdiction. Your base (home) jurisdiction will collect and transmit fees to other member jurisdictions or will issue a refund if you overpaid. Fuel tax audits are only performed by the base state.

Under this system, you must carefully plan and document your fuel us- age and purchases and miles traveled in each state. For example, if you purchase 100 gallons of fuel but only use 50 in that jurisdiction, you are due a fuel tax credit. If you used 100 gallons but purchased only 50 gallons of fuel in that jurisdiction, you owe tax.

Log Books & Trip Sheets & ELD

The use of a "trip sheet" (see next page) can help you stay organized and compliant with IFTA regulations. If you use a computer in your business, consider fuel reporting software to document your fuel purchases and miles driven. A compliance services can handle the permit and fuel reporting process for you, if you prefer. These services charge monthly fees ranging from $30 to $60.

Some truckers only operate in one state, and if you are one of them, you may consider filing the quarterly fuel tax returns on your own, savingmoney.

You may obtain the complete International Fuel Tax Agreement, Administrative Procedures and Audit Guidelines, from your base state's department of transportation motor vehicles division. You can also obtain information online.

Log Book and Trip Sheets: Part 395 of the Federal Motor Carrier Safety Regulations outlines the **Hours of Service of Drivers** and recording requirements. The regulations state that "every driver who operates a commercial motor vehicle shall record his/ her duty status, in duplicate, for each 24-hour period." Generally, truckers use a log book to comply with this requirement. In this log, you must record your driving, on-duty and off-duty, and sleeper berth times as well as number of other details. You must keep this log current because regulatory agencies such as the DOT or highway patrol may request to inspect it at any time. You can obtain log books at truck stops.

After each trip, you also must complete a trip sheet where you record the date, state, route or highway, and loaded or empty miles. You will need this information to file your road and fuel tax reports.

Owner- Operators must keep a copy of the FMCSR in their truck. The *Federal Motor Carrier Safety Regulations* pocketbook is published by J.J. Keller and Associates, and available at most truck stops.

All the above log book regulations will become outdated when the new ELD regulations become law on December 18, 2017.

Electronic Logging Devices to be Required Across Commercial Truck and Bus Industries.

WASHINGTON – The U.S. Department of Transportation's Federal Motor Carrier Safety Administration (FMCSA) today announced the adoption of a Final Rule that will improve roadway safety by employing technology to strengthen commercial truck and bus drivers' compliance with hours-of-service regulations that prevent fatigue.

"Since 1938, complex, on-duty/off-duty logs for truck and bus drivers were made with pencil and paper, virtually impossible to verify," said U.S. Transportation Secretary Anthony Foxx. "This automated technology not only brings logging records into the modern age, it also allows roadside safety inspectors to unmask violations of federal law that put lives at risk."

The Final Rule requiring the use of electronic logging devices (ELD) will result in an annual net benefit of more than $1 billion – largely by reducing the amount of required industry paperwork. It will also increase the efficiency of roadside law enforcement personnel in reviewing driver records. Strict protections are included that will protect commercial drivers from harassment.

On an annual average basis, the ELD Final Rule is estimated to save 26 lives and prevent 562 injuries resulting from crashes involving large commercial motor vehicles.

"This is a win for all motorists on our nation's roadways," said FMCSA Acting Administrator Scott Darling. "Employing technology to ensure that commercial drivers comply with federal hours-of-service rules will prevent crashes and save lives."

An ELD automatically records driving time. It monitors engine hours, vehicle movement, miles driven, and location information.

Federal safety regulations limit the number of hours commercial drivers can be on-duty and still drive, as well as the number of hours spent driving. These limitations are designed to prevent truck and bus drivers from becoming fatigued while driving, and require that drivers take a work break and have a sufficient off-duty rest period before returning to on-duty status.

The four main elements of the ELD Final Rule include:

- Requiring commercial truck and bus drivers who currently use paper log books to maintain hours-of-service records to adopt ELDs within two years. It is anticipated that approximately three million drivers will be impacted.
- Strictly prohibiting commercial driver harassment. The Final Rule provides both procedural and technical provisions designed to protect commercial truck and bus drivers from harassment resulting from information generated by ELDs. [A separate FMCSA rulemaking further safeguards commercial drivers from being coerced to violate federal safety regulations and provides the agency with the authority to take enforcement actions not only against motor carriers, but also against shippers, receivers, and transportation intermediaries.]
- Setting technology specifications detailing performance and design requirements for ELDs so that manufacturers are able to produce compliant devices and systems – and purchasers are enabled to make informed decisions.
- Establishing new hours-of-service supporting document (shipping documents, fuel purchase receipts, etc.) requirements that will result in additional paperwork reductions. In most cases, a motor carrier would not be required to retain supporting documents verifying on-duty driving time.

The ELD Final Rule permits the use of smart phones and other wireless devices as ELDs, so long as they satisfy technical specifications, are certified, and are listed on an FMCSA website. Canadian- and Mexican-domiciled drivers will also be required to use ELDs when operating on U.S. roadways.

Motor carriers who have previously installed compliant Automatic On-Board Recording Devices may continue to use the devices for an additional two years beyond the compliance date.

A copy of the ELD Final Rule announced today is available at: https://www.fmcsa.dot.gov/hours-service/elds/electronic-logging-devices-and-hours-service-supporting-documents.

Further information, including a comprehensive, searchable list of frequently asked questions, and a calendar of upcoming free training webinars, is available https://www.fmcsa.dot.gov/elds.

Our Information Package and Business Guide is based on experience and provides you with step-by-step information. We are sure it will be a valuable guide to help you start your own successful trucking business.

It explains the initial steps to become an Owner-Operator, the process of purchasing your own truck, and the lease-on process. Further, there is a financial section, information about fuel and road taxes, and details how to obtain your own operating authority.

Please study each step carefully. We are confident you soon will be a successful Owner-Operator.

Also, please remember to visit us on the Internet at www.truckingsuccess.com, where you will find additional useful services and products.

Our web site now features a business plan including financial projections for entrepreneurs who would like to start a trucking company. Modified to your specifications, this sample business plan may be presented to apply for an SBA loan.

The Author

TruckingSuccess.com

7054 North 28th Drive
Phoenix, AZ 85051

Tel. (602) 864-8056

Email:
support@truckingsuccess.com

Information presented in this brochure is current at the time of printing.
Specifications subject to change.
TX4-400-341

66317088R00035

Made in the USA
Middletown, DE
10 March 2018